EASY GUIDE TO STARTING A

DROP SHIPPING

BUSINESS

A DETAILED AND EASY GUIDE TO
UNDERSTANDING HOW TO START
MAKING MONEY FROM DROP SHIPPING
NOW

BY KEVIN SANTOS

TABLE OF CONTENTS

INTRODUCTION

IS THE DROP SHIPPING BUSINESS MODEL RIGHT FOR YOU?

There are many things to consider when you open a retail store, but among the most important considerations, you must decide if you want to store inventory or attain a wholesale distributor. If you choose to store inventory, you must purchase products in bulk, store, unpack and ship them to buyers of your products. However, by choosing a wholesale distributor, you can contract the process of storing, packing and shipping to a drop ship provider. A drop ship provider is also identified as direct fulfillment, but both terms can be used to describe the same service.

Dropshipping is a fast growing business model because of the low cost and simplicity in getting started. Once you understand the concept you will see why it is becoming such a popular way of doing business online.

With dropshipping, store owners can sell products to their customers without actually stocking the items themselves. Dropshipping isn't something new. Zappos started dropshipping back in 1999. Amazon and Sears use this business model, too. If big names don't catch your attention, look at the regular guys making their way and sharing their stories as dropshippers on Reddit. Nowadays, up to 33% of the entire ecommerce industry uses dropshipping as a primary inventory management model.

Small scale ecommerce entrepreneurs love dropshipping because there is no inventory to hold, which translates into a lower upfront investment. Not having to manage an inventory also lets you concentrate more on the most important thing – bringing in new customers.

The whole spectrum of doing business has undergone a world of change in the last few decades. One of the latest online business ideas is dropship services. This online business involves a process in which manufacturers or suppliers deliver the products directly to the customers of the dropship business without the business having to pre-purchase or stock the goods. The best part of the bargain is that the business owner, or reseller, does not have to do any hard work such as inventing, designing, buying or making the product, testing the market, describing the product on the website, making the website attractive, or promoting the product.

The dropship services business owner just has to list the products on eBay and get orders for the products by using its own or the supplying company's descriptions and graphics. When the orders are received, the reseller supplies the information regarding the buyers' names and addresses and other details of the order, so that the supplier can send the products to the buyer. The company also collects the payment.

The business of dropship services can reap rich returns for the business owner, but the most important dropshipping guide is that it is necessary to take care of the business and customers to ensure that any buyers' complaints regarding poor product quality or delays between receipt of payments and delivery of goods are tended to promptly. Any negligence in providing necessary after-sales services and attending to complaints can tarnish the image of the company and lead to loss of revenue and future orders. In order to find an answer to how to dropship and how to start a dropshipping business, it is vital to select a reliable supplier. The wrong selection can have disastrous results. Follow the following steps before starting this type of business.

1) Select Recommended Suppliers: The first step for starting a dropship services business is that the sourcing of the suppliers should be done with great care. Simply select the suppliers recommended by other people. It is possible to get free or paid-for lists of dropshipping companies on Internet directory sites. Some give accurate information

whereas others might be owned by unscrupulous suppliers, so avoid those particular recommendations.

2) Check the Contact Details: Once a selection is made based on reliable recommendations, and after checking that the range of products that the business intends to deal are sold by the supplier, check the contact details provided by the supplier. Pertinent contact information such as phone number, email address, and a mailing address should be available on the supplier's website. Avoid any supplier with incorrect or with no contact information at all. Make sure the phone is answered and see how long it takes for the supplier to answer emails, which may come in handy later if you have a reason to contact them with a problem.

3) Check Business Terms: Since there can be disputes with the supplier regarding faulty goods or undelivered items, business terms and conditions of the supplier should be properly stated and understood by the reseller. Realize that the responsibilities of the business as a reseller are different than the responsibilities that the supplier would have toward the reseller.

4) Unreasonable Subscription Fees: As a reseller, the dropship services business has to pay resellers registration fees and, in some cases, ongoing subscription charges for the right to access the supplier's catalogue. Access for a limited time is normally allowed before

registration. Before registering with any supplier, check whether it charges ongoing subscription fees. Fine print should also be checked well for any between-the-lines clauses.

5) Beware of Middlemen Disguised as Suppliers: Check whether the potential supplier holds enough stock of the products and they are not a middleman posing as a supplier. These middlemen place orders with the real supplier and when they receive orders from the reseller and, in this process, long delays can take place. These delays can result in losses to the customer and subsequent losses to the reseller because the payment would have to be refunded.

6) Modes of Payment: Find out how the supplier expects to receive payments because the most convenient mode would be the same by which the customer pays the reseller. This will save charges and time. It is also advisable to avoid having to pay by Wire Transfer or Telegraph Transfer because the risk is higher if there is no customer protection.

7) Beware of Companies Selling Fake Goods: While choosing a supplier, avoid those sites that offer branded goods such as designer clothing and electrical goods at unbelievably low prices. Such low priced, so-called designer goods are bound to be fake unless the supplier is trustworthy and renowned and he has obtained the goods from a close-out, or if the goods are refurbished or Grade A returns. If

the reseller sells fake goods, he can be accused of selling counterfeit goods.

8) Look for Web Reviews: Having short-listed a few suppliers, it would be helpful to seek out reviews and comments regarding the companies on Internet forums from other dropship resellers. Although it might be difficult to find any good comments since the resellers would not like others to know about their profitable source, bad reviews can certainly help in making the right decision.

9) Look for Artists and Craftsmen: Teaming up with artists and craftsmen for their creative products is a unique way to do dropship services business. These creative people usually lack marketing savvy. Visits to local craft fairs can provide unlimited opportunities to get stunning creative items at unbelievably low prices as compared to eBay prices. The dropship business need not buy these items, but an arrangement could be worked out for working on commission. They will likely be happy to take his payment and deliver the products to the buyer of the dropship business when a sale is made.

CHAPTER 1

SO WHAT IS DROP SHIPPING

Drop shipping is a retail method in which you don't keep products in stock. Instead, you partner with a wholesale supplier that stocks its own inventory - you transfer customer orders and shipment details to them, and they ship the goods directly to the customer. The biggest benefit of drop shipping is you don't have to worry about fulfillment or inventory issues.

Drop shipping is a way to sell physical products without having a storefront or having to buy inventory in bulk but still getting a wholesale price from your supplier. Drop shippers can sell everything from t-shirts to TVs.

Dropshipping is a retail fulfillment method where a store doesn't keep the products it sells in stock. Instead, when a store sells a product, it purchases the item from a third party and has it shipped directly to the customer. As a result, the merchant never sees or handles the product.

The biggest difference between dropshipping and the standard retail model is that the selling merchant doesn't stock or own inventory. Instead, the merchant purchases inventory as needed from a third party – usually a wholesaler or manufacturer – to fulfill orders.

Traditional, brick and mortar retailers, like Best Buy, have stores that they fill with inventory. They buy the inventory in bulk from suppliers, say 10,000 TVs from Sony. In exchange for buying the products in bulk, suppliers charge retailers a lower, wholesale price, say $400 per TV. Retailers make their money by marking up those products before selling them to their customers. Best Buy sells the TV they bought from Sony for $400 to their customer for $750. Best Buy just made $350.

Drop shippers also sell a physical product to their customer, again, lets say it's a $750 TV. And they've also marked up the price from the wholesale price they paid to their supplier, again, we'll say it's $400. The drop shipper just made $350. But here's the difference, the drop shipper didn't buy 10,000 TVs from the supplier – they bought one. This begs the question, if drop shippers don't buy their inventory in bulk like Best Buy, how can they get wholesale prices like Best Buy?

Keys To Successfully Drop Shipping

While drop-shipping can be a great way to provide excellent customer service, manage your warehouse space effectively, and test new products, there are three things you need to keep in mind in order to have the most success possible.

Does your order management system generate purchase orders for your drop-ship suppliers? If you do not have an order management solution in place, or if the solution you do have in place doesn't have processes built-in to help you drop-ship orders, it is a good idea to look into upgrading your system. If you have to manually create purchase orders for your suppliers to drop-ship products to your customers, you may lose much of the benefit of drop-shipping in time spent. The best order management systems have built-in processes to automatically generate drop-ship purchase orders and submit them to your suppliers.

Are you able to sell these items and maintain margins? Most drop-ship suppliers will charge more to send an order directly to your customer than they will to ship products to your warehouse. This is typically due to volume discounts that you receive when purchasing large orders of products you intend to stock and ship from your location. The supplier typically receives a shipping discount for shipping in bulk, and they pass some of that savings along to you. However, when you ask that they send a product directly to your customer, they often have a higher cost for the item and a higher shipping fee that they also pass along to you. Know the difference in margin and make your drop-shipping choices accordingly.

Remember your drop-ship suppliers offer the same service to other merchants. This means that even if you are able to get daily product availability updates from your suppliers, you must keep in mind that these products are available to many other merchants. It is not a good idea to consider these products as 100% available. Make sure that you work with drop-ship suppliers who have large available quantities of their products or can get more quickly. You don't want to have upset customers waiting for weeks to receive the items they bought from you. This is also the reason that it is not recommended to offer products for sale on major marketplaces such as Amazon and eBay if you will only be having them drop-shipped. If your supplier runs out of stock, they won't be able to fulfill your customers' orders. This can have a negative impact on your seller ratings and can even lead to your accounts being suspended or shut down.

Benefits

Less Capital Is Required – Probably the biggest advantage to dropshipping is that it's possible to launch an ecommerce store without having to invest thousands of dollars in inventory up front. Traditionally, retailers have had to tie up huge amounts of capital purchasing inventory.

With the dropshipping model, you don't have to purchase a product unless you already made the sale and have been paid by the customer. Without major up-front inventory investments, it's possible to start a successful dropshipping business with very little money.

Easy to Get Started – Running an ecommerce business is much easier when you don't have to deal with physical products. With dropshipping, you don't have to worry about:

Managing or paying for a warehouse

Packing and shipping your orders

Tracking inventory for accounting reasons

Handling returns and inbound shipments

Continually ordering products and managing stock level

Low Overhead – Because you don't have to deal with purchasing inventory or managing a warehouse, your overhead expenses are quite low. In fact, many successful dropshipping businesses are run from a home office with a laptop for less than $100 per month. As you grow, these expenses will likely increase but will still be low compared to those of traditional brick-and-mortar businesses.

Flexible Location – A dropshipping business can be run from just about anywhere with an internet connection. As long as you can communicate with suppliers and customers easily, you can run and manage your business.

Wide Selection of Products – Because you don't have to pre-purchase the items you sell, you can offer an array of products to your potential customers. If suppliers stock an item, you can list if for sale on your website at no additional cost.

Easy to Scale – With a traditional business, if you receive three times as much business you'll usually need to do three times as much work. By leveraging dropshipping suppliers, most of the work to process additional orders will be borne by the suppliers, allowing you to expand with fewer growing pains and less incremental work. Sales growth will always bring additional work – especially related to customer service – but business that utilize dropshipping scale particularly well relative to traditional ecommerce businesses.

All these benefits make dropshipping a very attractive model to both beginning and established merchants. Unfortunately, dropshipping isn't all roses and rainbows. All this convenience and flexibility comes at a price.

Why Do Suppliers Give Drop Shippers A Special Deal?

Suppliers offer the drop shipper such a special deal because the supplier isn't a name brand – they aren't Sony.

A supplier with a popular brand, like Sony, can demand that retailers buy their product in bulk. Traditional retailers will agree because they know Sony products have regular customers and the products will sell. Sony's brand makes their products safe for retailers to buy in bulk so Sony doesn't need to make special deals with drop shippers.

But what about an unknown brand, like SuperDuperFuture TVs? They aren't a name brand so traditional retailers don't know if customers will buy their products. If a retailer doesn't know if a brand will sell, they are unlikely to risk buying a bunch of it in bulk. Without traditional retailers to buy their products in bulk, SuperDuperFuture TVs will be more likely to make special deals with drop shippers.

 This isn't a one sided deal though! With a good drop shipping partner, the supplier doesn't have to spend a fortune on marketing trying to develop a brand before selling their products. Drop shippers are experts at marketing, sales, and customer service. So by making a deal with a drop shipper the supplier gains access to a retailer who can successfully introduce their brand to customers.

Is Drop Shipping A Profitable Business Model?

Drop shipping model that I used to start my own store after quitting my job and build a seven-figure business. So it's definitely possible to build meaningful drop shipping businesses that generate real wealth. However this was in 2008.

Since then, it's become more difficult to compete as a drop shipper in the world of Amazon and as eCommerce has become more competitive. Today, it's important to have a very strong unique selling proposition. It's not impossible to accomplish this with drop shipping, but this is much harder when you're selling other people's products.

Drop shipping usually works best when you can a) offer a tremendous amount of informational value with your products and b) you can sell a lot of high-margin accessories or c) you use it to supplement a catalog of your own proprietary products.

What Kind Of Profit Margins Can I Expect With Drop Shipping?

Profit margins will vary greatly depending on the products you sell. For expensive electronics, margins are thin and will likely be in the 5% to 10% range. But for low-priced accessories, margins will often be in the 100% range.

However, on average drop shipping gross margins are usually in the 10% to 15% range.

Where Do People Sell Drop Shipped Products?

People sell drop shipped products just about everywhere! Many sales on eBay and Amazon are fulfilled through drop shippers, as are items on thousands of eCommerce sites, especially smaller ones.

And even the big boys utilize drop shipping to expand their product catalog and offerings. It's likely that large companies like Sears and Home Depot utilize the drop shipping model for some of their less popular items. This allows them to offer a broad selection while limiting the inventory they have to maintain.

While it's possible to sell drop shipped items in a number of ways, creating your own eCommerce site offers the best chance of building a scalable, profitable and successful business in the long run.

Disadvantages

Low Margins – Low margins are the biggest disadvantage to operating in a highly competitive dropshipping niche. Because it's so easy to get started – and the overhead costs are so minimal – many merchants will set up shop and sell items at rock-bottom prices in an attempt to grow revenue. They've invested so little in getting the business started so they can afford to operate on minuscule margins.

True, these merchants often have low-quality websites and poor (if any) customer service. But that won't stop customers from comparing their prices to yours. This increase in cutthroat competition will quickly destroy the profit margin in a niche. Fortunately, you can do a lot to mitigate this problem by selecting a niche that's well suited for dropshipping.

Inventory Issues – If you stock all your own items, it's relatively simple to keep track of which items are in and out of stock. But when you're sourcing from multiple warehouses, which are also fulfilling orders for other merchants, inventory changes on a daily basis. While there are ways you can better sync your store's inventory with your suppliers', these solutions don't always work seamlessly, and suppliers don't always support the technology required.

Shipping Complexities – If you work with multiple suppliers – as most drop shippers do – the products on your website will be sourced through a number of different drop shippers. This complicates your shipping costs.

Let's say a customer places an order for three items, all of which are available only from separate suppliers. You'll incur three separate shipping charges for sending each item to the customer, but it's probably not wise to pass this charge along to the customer, as they'll think you're grossly overcharging for shipping! And even if you did want to pass these charges along, automating these calculations can be difficult.

Supplier Errors – Have you ever been blamed for something that wasn't your fault, but you had to accept responsibility for the mistake anyway?

Even the best dropshipping suppliers make mistakes fulfilling orders – mistakes for which you have to take responsibility and apologize. And mediocre and low-quality suppliers will cause endless frustration with missing items, botched shipments and low-quality packing, which can damage your business's reputation.

Common Problems With Drop Shipping

Despite my glowing recommendation, drop shipping isn't ecommerce nirvana. Like all models, it has its weaknesses and downsides. With some planning and awareness, these issues can be managed and need not prevent you from running a successful drop shipping business.

1. There Will Be Loads Of Competition And Awful Margins.

Solution: It's true. Products that can be drop shipped will spawn a lot of competition. Usually this will lead to cutthroat pricing and diminishing profit margins, making it hard to build a viable business.

To be successful, you typically can't compete on price. Instead, you'll need to offer value in a different way, usually through top-notch product education, service or selection.

2. Syncing Inventory Is Difficult & Leads To Out-Of-Stock Items.

Solution: The best way to mitigate this problem is to work with multiple suppliers with overlapping product lines. It's inherently dangerous to rely on a single supplier. Having two suppliers doubles the likelihood that an item will be in stock and available for shipment.

Many sophisticated suppliers offer a real-time product feed, and you can use a service like eCommHub to easily sync your Shopify website with the warehouse.

Eventually, you'll sell a customer an out-of-stock item. Instead of canceling the order, give the customer an upgraded product for free! You might not make much – if any – money on the order, but you'll likely build a loyal brand advocate.

3. It's Hard To Sell Products That You Never See.

Solution: In today's world, it's possible to become an expert in just about everything through information online. Selling products from manufacturers with detailed websites will allow you to become intimately familiar with a product line without ever having touched a physical item. And when you do need to answer specific question about a product, a quick call to your supplier or manufacturer will give you the answer you need.

You can also buy your most popular items to get acquainted with them, and then resell them as "used" or "refurbished," often recouping most of your investment.

4. Involving A Third Party Will Result In More Fulfillment Errors, Mistakes, And Logistical Problems.

Solution: Even the best drop shippers make occasional mistakes, and mediocre ones make a lot of them. Suppliers are fairly good about paying to remedy problems, but when they're not, you need to be willing to spend what's necessary to resolve the issue for your customer.

If you try to blame your supplier for a fulfillment problem, you're going to come off as amateurish and unprofessional. Similarly, if you're unwilling to ship out a cheap replacement part to a customer because your supplier won't cover the cost, your reputation is going to suffer.

One of the costs of drop shipping convenience is the expense of remedying logistical problems. If you accept it as cost of doing business – and always make sure to put your customer first – it shouldn't be a long-term issue.

CHAPTER 2

GETTING STARTED

The idea of drop shipping is that a wholesale drop shipper (the supplier) offers you the option of selling products without buying them first. They also act as service providers who prevent you from having to:

Store items

Package and ship items

Risk money on items when you aren't sure about how they will sell

But they don't do all that for free! When you buy from a wholesaler offering drop shipping services, they add a fee to cover the costs involved with offering this service.

This is usually US$2-US$5 per item, which means you must be careful when you think about the products you want to drop ship, as there are some items which are much more suitable for drop shipping than others. We suggest going for:

Deep niches such as rear brake lights for late model Honda Civics

Low-volume sell-through rates and high profit margins – meaning you won't sell 150 per week but you will make a decent profit on them when they do sell

Low competition. This is important when you are drop shipping as you have to take those drop shipping fees into consideration, which makes keeping up in a competitive market really tough on sellers who are drop shipping.

1: Find A Supplier

You need to explore a few different possible suppliers. Try our own SaleHoo Directory which is full of reputable sellers stocking a wide range of products from cosmetics to farming equipment.

For local suppliers, try flicking through your Yellow Pages in the Wholesale or Suppliers sections. Look for ones who have plenty of experience in drop shipping and who understand the importance of sending out your items in a timely manner.

Before negotiating a deal with them, ask:

How long it will take for an order to be shipped once you have placed the order with them?

What shipping methods do they offer? E.g. overnight courier, or for international suppliers, which company they use and what their tracking systems are like.

 What are their quality control systems? You don't want to be dealing with sub-standard products, it will mean lots of hassles with returns, which wastes valuable time you could spend on making money.

Do they offer warranties?

Can you use their product photos? Large wholesalers often have professional product photos taken which will make your listings all the more professional looking

 2: Select Products And Find The Best Selling Ones

Those who know exactly what they want to sell. Start by trawling through your suppliers product range and pick out a few items which interest you and do some market research. Find the best selling items by:

Using a service like SaleHoo Market Research Lab, which performs market research for you when you input key words into the search tool, and tells you all sorts of valuable information including the average selling price, average shipping price and sell-through rate (ratio of listings which sell in relation to those which do not). It's free with your SaleHoo membership, well worth it to ensure you choose only profitable items to sell!

OR The old fashioned way: Taking a close look through eBay's completed listings. If you haven't used this method before, follow these:

Go to eBay.com (or your local eBay site)

Click 'advanced search' (located right next to eBay's search bar)

Check the 'completed listings' box

Enter your keywords and category and hit the search button

Now scroll through around 5 pages of listings and count the number of successful listings (listed in green), compared to the unsuccessful ones (listed in red).

When you find an item which sells 60% (or more) of the time you can be pretty certain that you will be successful in selling it. The easiest way to find out whether a product sells 60% (or more) is to scroll right down to the bottom of the page and make sure you're viewing 50 items per page. Then go through and count the number of green listings. When you get to the bottom and have counted at least 30 (60%) green listings out of the 50 listed... that's a good sign! You might be onto something so keep looking through a few more pages to make sure.

If none of your products match up, go back and find something else to research or try searching the same product under different key words and categories.

3: Get A Tax ID

Not all eBay sellers need a tax ID (also known as retail or resellers license, tax ID, resale number resale certificate or vendor's license) but some wholesale suppliers require you to have one before they will do business with you.

You need to get a sales tax ID if you are inside the US or Canada and running a business (not just selling items from around the home).

Note that some US states including Alaska, Delaware, Montana, New Hampshire and Oregon do not require sales tax IDs. So let your wholesaler know if that's the case, as they may have another form for you to fill out.

Applying for a tax ID is easy and inexpensive; you can do it by visiting your local county clerk's office or online – just Google "[your state] + sales tax ID".

To get a sales tax ID, you may need to be a business entity; a company or a sole proprietor (which applies to a lot of at-home online businesses), and to have a Federal Tax ID number.

4: Choose A Selling Platform

The obvious selling platform is eBay but there are plenty of other online auction sites out there which are growing rapidly and getting a lot of traffic (and some are even fee-free or much cheaper to use than eBay!)

Check out sites like Bonanza.com or Amazon.com and see if there is a market there for your product range. It's a good idea to diversify when it comes to selling on online auction sites as each site has its own unique visitors (not everyone checks eBay first!) and with most sites being free to join, there is no reason not to give others a try.

For sellers who are really looking to diversify, consider setting up your own eCommerce site such as a SaleHoo Store which is the fastest and easiest way to open your own store. You can get a free 30 day trial of SaleHoo Stores right now and try it for yourself.

5: Manage Your Listings

When drop shipping, you will list your items in the same way you would if you had the stock on hand, but when selling on eBay (and some other sites, you must check individual policies), you must disclose in your listing to all potential buyers the location of your item.

For example, if your supplier is based in Hong Kong, you must display this in your listing so that buyers are aware that there may be longer than expected shipping times.

Drop shipping orders work a little differently than regular wholesale orders. Here's what a typical drop ship order will look like:

After you have chosen your items from your supplier, you will list them on eBay or on your eCommerce site (also read: Amazon Webstore vs. BigCommerce vs. Shopify).

Once the item is sold, you will collect the money from the buyer and pay your supplier (keeping the profit you make, of course!) by ordering the item you have just sold from their website

The supplier will then send out the item you have sold directly to your buyer. You will soon work out which products have a great sell-through rate and which don't and can begin adjusting which products you list accordingly.

CHAPTER 3

THE SUPPLY CHAIN & FULFILLMENT PROCESS

"Supply chain" is a fancy term describing the path a product takes to go from conception through manufacturing and finally into the hands of a customer. If we were talking with hard-core supplier chain gurus, they'd insist a product's supply chain reaches all the way to the mining of the materials (like oil and rubber) used to manufacture an item. But that's a little intense.

For the purposes of this guide, we don't need to get quite that detailed. You simply need to understand the three most applicable players that make up the dropshipping supply chain: manufacturers, wholesalers and retailers.

Manufacturers – Manufacturers create the product and most do not sell directly to the public. Instead, they sell in bulk to wholesalers and retailers.

Buying directly from the manufacturer is the cheapest way to purchase products for resale, but most have minimum purchase requirements you'll need to meet. You'll also need to stock and then re-ship the products when selling them to customers. For these reasons, it's often easier to buy directly from a wholesaler.

Wholesalers – Wholesalers buy products in bulk from manufacturers, mark them up slightly and then sell them to retailers for resale to the public. If they do have purchasing minimums, they're generally much lower than those required by a manufacturer.

Wholesalers will usually stock products from dozens – if not hundreds – of manufacturers and tend to operate in a specific industry or niche. Most are strictly wholesaler operators, meaning they sell only to retailers and not directly to the general public.

Retailers – A retailer is anyone who sells products directly to the public at a markup. If you run a business that fulfills your orders via dropshipping suppliers, you're a retailer.

Dropshipping Is A Service, Not A Role

You'll notice that "dropshipper" isn't one of the players listed in the supply chain. Why? Because any of the three – manufacturer, wholesaler or retailer – can act as a drop shipper!

If a manufacturer is willing to ship its products directly to your customer, it is "dropshipping" on your behalf. Similarly, a retail merchant can offer to dropship, although its pricing won't be as competitive as a wholesaler's because it isn't buying directly from the manufacturer.

Just because someone claims to be a "dropshipper" does not mean you're getting wholesale pricing. It simply means the company will ship products on your behalf. To get the best pricing, you want to make sure you're working directly with a legitimate wholesaler or manufacturer, a topic we'll be covering in-depth in the next chapter.

Dropshipping in Action: The Order Process

Now that you understand the players involved, let's take a look at how a drop shipped order gets processed. To illustrate, we'll follow an order placed with our theoretical store, Phone Outlet, an online merchant that specializes in accessories for smart phones. Phone Outlet dropships all of its products directly from a wholesaler we'll call Wholesale Accessories.

Here's a sample of how the entire ordering process might look:

Customer Places Order With Phone Outlet

Mr. Allen needs a case for his new smartphone and places an order via Phone Outlet's online store. Once the order is approved, a few things happen:

Phone Outlet and Mr. Allen get an email confirmation (likely identical) of the new order that is automatically generated by the store software.

Mr. Allen's payment is captured during the checkout process and will be automatically deposited into Phone Outlet's bank account.

Phone Accessory Outlet Places the Order With Its Supplier

This step is usually as simple as Phone Outlet forwarding the email order confirmation to a sales representative at Wholesale Accessories. Wholesale Accessories has Phone Outlet's credit card on file and will bill it for the wholesale price of the goods, including any shipping or processing fees.

Note: Some sophisticated dropshippers will support automatic XML (a common format for inventory files) order uploading or the ability to place the order manually online, but email is the most common way to place orders with dropshipping suppliers because it's universal and easy to use.

Wholesale Accessories Ships The Order

Assuming the item is in stock and the wholesaler was able to successfully charge Phone Outlet's card, Wholesale Accessories will box up the order and ship it directly to the customer. Though the shipment comes from Wholesale Accessories, Phone Outlet's name and address will appear on the return address label and its logo will appear on the invoice and packing slip. Once the shipment has been finalized, Wholesale Accessories will email an invoice and a tracking number to Phone Outlet.

Note: The turnaround time on dropshipped orders is often faster than you'd think. Most quality suppliers will be able to get an order out the door in a few hours, allowing merchants to advertise same-day shipping even when they are using a dropshipping supplier.

Phone Outlet Alerts The Customer Of Shipment

Once the tracking number is received, Phone Outlet will send the tracking information to the customer, likely using an email interface that's built in to the online store interface. With the order shipped, the payment collected and the customer notified, the order and fulfillment process is complete. Phone Outlet's profit (or loss) is the difference between what it charged Mr. Allen and what it paid Wholesale Accessories.

Dropshippers Are Invisible

Despite its critical role in the ordering and fulfillment process, the dropshipper is completely invisible to the end customer. When the package is received, only Phone Outlet's return address and logo will be on the shipment. If Mr. Allen's receives the wrong case, he would contact Phone Outlet, which would then coordinate behind the scenes with Wholesale Accessories to get the right item sent out.

The dropshipping wholesaler doesn't exist to the end customer. Its sole responsibility is to stock and ship products. Everything else – marketing, website development, customer service, etc. – is the responsibility of the merchant.

CHAPTER 4

PICKING PRODUCTS TO DROP SHIP

The biggest hurdle most new dropshipping entrepreneurs face is picking a niche and products to focus on. And it's understandable – it's likely the biggest decision you'll make and has long-term consequences on the success or failure of the business.

The most common mistake at this stage is picking a product based on personal interest or passion. This is an acceptable strategy if being interested in the product is your primary objective, not necessarily business success. But if your #1 goal is to build a profitable dropshipping site, you'll want to consider setting your personal passions aside when doing market research, or at least making sure they meet with the criteria discussed below.

How To Be Successful Selling Online

To build a successful ecommerce business, you'll need to do one of the following:

Manufacture Your Own Product – You control distribution and are the sole source for the item. This limits competition and allows you to charge a premium price. If you intend to dropship products, you'll be selling existing products manufactured by someone else, so this isn't an option.

Have Access to Exclusive Pricing or Distribution – If you can arrange an exclusive agreement to carry a product – or if you have access to exclusive pricing from a manufacturer – you can profitably sell online without creating your own product. These arrangements can be difficult to arrange, however, and hundreds of other dropship merchants will have access to similar goods and wholesale prices.

Sell at the Lowest Price – If you can offer the lowest price, you'll likely steal business from a large chunk of the market. The only problem? It's a business model doomed to failure. If the only thing of value you have to offer is a low price, you'll be caught in a pricing war that will strip virtually all your profits. Trying to compete against Amazon and other established online giants on price is generally a poor strategy.

Add Value in Non-Pricing Terms – Offering valuable information that complements your products is the BEST way to differentiate yourself and charge a premium price. Entrepreneurs set out to solve people's problems, and that's no different in the world of ecommerce and dropshipping. Offering expert advice and guidance within your niche is the best way to build a profitable dropshipping business.

Adding Value in Ecommerce – Just add value! Simple enough, right? Well, that's easier said than done. Some products and niches lend themselves to this strategy more than others. You should look for a few key characteristics that make adding value with educational content much easier.

High Quality Product Images - You'll need to make sure customers get a good sense of the product and that starts with high quality product images. Check out Burst for free product photos. It also features some business ideas you can use to get your store up and running.

Have Many Components – The more components a product needs to function properly, the more likely customers are to turn to the internet for answers. Which purchase is more confusing: buying a new office chair or buying a home security camera system that requires multiple cameras, complex wiring and a recorder?

The more components a product needs – and the more variety among those components – the greater your opportunity to add value by advising customers on which products are compatible.

Are Customizable/Confusing – Along the same vein, confusing and customizable products are perfect for adding value through content. Would you inherently know how to select the best hot water solar panel configuration for your climate or which type of wireless dog collar system is right for your yard? Being able to offer specific guidance on what types of products are best suited for specific environments and customers is a great way to add value.

Require Technical Setup or Installation – It's easy to offer expert guidance for products that are difficult to set up, install or assemble. Take the security camera system from before. Let's say the camera site had a detailed 50-page installation guide that also covered the most common mistakes people make installing their own systems. If you thought the guide could save you time and hassle, there's a good chance you'd buy it from that website even if it was available for a few dollars less elsewhere. For store owners, the guides add tremendous value to customers and don't cost anything to provide once they're created.

Ways To Add Value:

You can add value to complex and confusing niches in a number of ways, including:

Creating comprehensive buyers' guides

Investing in detailed product descriptions and listings

Creating installation and setup guides (as discussed above)

Creating in-depth videos showing how the product works

Establishing an easy-to-follow system for understanding component compatibility

Cherry-Picking the Best Customers

All customers aren't created equally. It's strange how some customers buying small items feel entitled to demand the moon while other big spenders rarely ask for anything.

Targeting the right demographic can be a big boon for your business. These clients tend to make it worth your while:

Hobbyists – People love their hobbies and will spend mind-boggling amounts on equipment, training and tools for them. Many serious mountain bikers have bikes that cost more than their cars, and folks who love to fish might spend a fortune outfitting their boats. If you can target the right hobbyist niche and successfully connect with enthusiasts and their needs, you can do very well.

Businesses – Business clients are sometimes more price-sensitive but will almost always order in larger quantities than individual consumers. Once you've established a rapport and earned their trust, you open the door to a long-term, high-volume profitable relationship. If at all possible, try to sell products that appeal to both individual customers and businesses.

Repeat Buyers – Recurring revenue is a beautiful thing. If you sell products that are disposable and/or need to be reordered frequently, you can grow rapidly as you build a loyal customer base that frequently returns to purchase.

Other Considerations When Selecting Products

The Perfect Price – Make sure you strongly consider the price point relative to the level of pre-sale service you'll need to provide. Most people feel comfortable placing a $200 order online without talking to someone on the phone. But what about a $1,500 item they're unfamiliar with? Chances are, most would want to chat directly with a sales representative before making such a large purchase, both to ensure the item is a good fit and to make sure the store is legitimate.

If you plan to sell high-priced items, make sure you're able to offer personalized phone support. You'll also want to ensure that the margins are rich enough to justify the pre-sale support you'll need to offer. Often, the $50 to $200 price range is the sweet spot to maximize revenue without having to provide extensive pre-sale support.

MAP Pricing – Some manufacturers will set what's called a minimum advertised price (MAP) for their products, and require that all resellers price their products at or above certain levels. This pricing floor prevents the price wars that often break out – especially for products that are easily drop shipped – and helps ensure that merchants can make a reasonable profit by carrying a manufacturer's products.

If you can find a niche where manufacturers enforce MAP pricing it's a huge benefit, especially if you plan on building a high-value and information-rich site. With prices the same across all competitors, you can compete on the strength of your website and won't have to worry about losing business to less reputable but cheaper competition.

Marketing Potential – The time to think about how you'll market a business is before you launch it, not three months in when you realize that customer acquisition is a nightmare. Can you brainstorm a number of ways you could promote your store by, for example, writing articles, giving away products or reaching out to active online communities that use the products you're selling? If not, you may want to reconsider.

Lots of Accessories – As a general rule of retail, margins on lower priced accessories are significantly higher than those of high-priced items. While a cell phone store may only make a 5% margin on the latest smartphone, they'll almost certainly make a 100% or 200% margin on the case that goes with it.

As customers, we're also much more sensitive about the price on a big-ticket item and care less about the price of smaller accessories. To use the previous example, you'd likely shop around for the best price on an expensive smartphone. But are you going to call around to find the best price on a $20 to $30 case? Probably not. You'll likely purchase it from the same store where you bought the phone.

Low Turnover – We hope you're convinced by now that investing in an education-rich, high-quality site will pay big dividends. But if the products you sell change every year, maintaining that site is quickly going to turn into a mountain of work. Try to find products that aren't updated with new models every year. That way, the time and money you invest in a superb site will last longer.

Hard to Find Locally – Selling a product that's hard to find locally will increase your chances of success as long as you don't get too specific. Most people needing a garden rake or a sprinkler would simply run down to the local hardware store. But where would you buy a medieval knight's costume or falcon training equipment? You'd probably head to Google and start searching.

Smaller Is Usually Better – In a world where free shipping is often expected, it can be a challenge to sell large, heavy equipment that's expensive to ship. The smaller the items, the easier they are to ship cheaply to your customers.

Picking a profitable niche isn't easy and requires you to consider numerous factors. These guidelines should give you a good idea of the types of drop shipped products that work well. For more on these attributes, please see this extended article on picking a profitable dropshipping niche.

Measuring Demand

Without demand, it doesn't matter if your niche fits 100% of the attributes listed above. If nobody wants your product, you'll have a hard time making any money! As the old saying goes, it's much easier to fill existing demand than to try to create it.

Fortunately, a number of online tools allow you to measure demand for a product or market. The most well-known and popular is the Google Keyword Tool.

Google Keyword Tool

The best way to measure demand for an item online is to see how many people are searching for it using a search engine like Google. Fortunately, Google makes this search volume publicly available via its keyword tool. Simply type in a word or phrase, and the tool tells you how many people are searching for it every month.

There are entire training modules dedicated to using the keyword tool, and we're not able to cover the tool exhaustively in this resource. But keep the following three tips in mind, and you'll be well on your way to getting the most out of the tool:

Match Type – The tool will let you select broad, phrase or exact match types when it reports search volumes. Unless you have a good reason to do otherwise, you should use the exact match option. This will give you a much more accurate picture of the applicable search volume for the keyword. For a more detailed explanation, see this article on understanding match types.

Search Location – Make sure you look at the difference between local search volume (in your country or a user-defined region) and global search volumes. If you'll be selling primarily in the U.S., you should focus on the local search volumes and ignore the global results, as that's where most of your customers will be.

Long-Tail Variations – It's easy to fixate on the broad, one- or two-word search terms that get massive amounts of search volume. In reality, it's the longer, more specific and lower volume search queries that will make up most of your traffic from the search engines. These longer, more detailed search terms are commonly referred to as "long-tail" searches.

Keep this in mind when you're looking at potential markets and niches to enter. If a search term has many variations that are actively searched for, that's a good sign that the market is fairly deep with lots of variety and interest. But if search queries and related volume drop off precipitously after the first few high-level words, there's probably less related long-tail traffic.

Google Trends

The keyword tool is great for raw search figures, but for more detailed insights you'll want to use Google Trends. The tool offers you information that the Keyword Tool just doesn't provide, including:

Search Volume Over Time: Ideally, you want the niche you're entering to be growing and Trends can let you know if this is the case. For any given search query, you can see the growth or decline in search volume over time. Below is a chart of search volume for the term "smartphone". As expected, search volume has risen sharply in the last few years:

Top and Rising Terms: You'll also be able to get a snapshot at the most popular related searches, and which queries have been growing in popularity the fastest. Focusing on these popular and quickly growing terms can be helpful when planning your marketing and SEO efforts. According to the charts below, search queries related to AT&T, Verizon and Samsung seem to be experiencing the most growth in the smart phone market – data which shows up when we analyze the term "smartphone":

Geographical Concentration: Another useful feature is the ability to see where people are searching for a term geographically. This can help you identify where your customer base for a niche is most heavily concentrated. For example, if you're selling canoes the charts below can help you determine that the majority of your customers will likely come from the Northern U.S., Alaska and Hawaii. If you were trying to decide between multiple suppliers, this knowledge could help you partner with one closest to the majority of your customers:

Seasonality: Understanding the seasonality of a market – that is, if the demand for a product changes dramatically at different points in the year – is crucially important. Because the keyword tool provides data on a monthly basis, you can draw some misleading conclusions if you measure search volumes during the wrong time of year.

Revisiting our previous example, we can see below that "canoes" are a very seasons search term with demand peaking in the summer months. If you measured demand in the summer expecting that it would be constant throughout the year, you'd grossly overestimate the size of demand:

For any product you're seriously considering, you'll want to spend time understanding the intricacies of the niche's search volume. Using the Google Trend tool to understand search volumes, geographic concentration, high-level search trends and seasonality will offer insights that can help you avoid costly mistakes and optimize your marketing efforts.

Measuring Competition

Conducting competitive analysis on a potential market can be tricky. Too much competition and you'll have difficulty building traffic and competing with established players. Too little competition can indicate a tiny market that will drastically limit how big you'll be able to grow.

Some dropshipping stores use paid advertising, but most will rely heavily on free traffic from the search engines to build a profitable business model. With this in mind, the best way to measure the overall competition in a market is to examine the organically listed (i.e., not advertised) sites on the first page of Google for a specific term. In order to generate a decent level of traffic, you'll need to successfully compete with (i.e., outrank) the sites on Google's first page.

The world of search engine optimization (SEO) is one we can't do justice in this dropshipping guide. For a more detailed discussion, we highly recommend SEOmoz's comprehensive "Beginner's Guide to SEO" or this more focused 15-minute SEO guide. But for the sake of evaluating competition, these four metrics will help you quickly gauge how strong the field is – and how hard it will be to outrank your competitors and generate traffic.

Number of Linking Domains

Google's ranking algorithm relies heavily on links. All else equal, the more links a site receives the higher it will rank in the search results. Knowing how many links are pointing to a site will give you an idea of how much work you'll need to do (in terms of earning and building links to your own site) to outrank your competitor.

There are dozens of different SEO metrics that are commonly used, but one in particularly is useful when evaluating the ranking strength of a site: the number of unique domains that link to it. Often called "linking root domains" or "unique linking domains", this metric represents the number of unique domains (ie independent sources) that link to a site and ignores duplicate links from the same domain.

To best understand this concept it's helpful to think of links like personal recommendations. If your best friend comes to you and recommends a restaurant, you may remember it. And if he raves about it every day for a week (a total of seven recommendations) you'll likely be moved to eat there. But even his fanaticism wouldn't be nearly as powerful as if seven unique, unrelated friends highly recommended the restaurant. Because they're independent sources, their recommendations hold much more authority.

The same is true when analyzing links to a site. A domain can link to a site repeatedly, but it's really one "unique" recommendation, and this is where common SEO metrics like "total number of links" can paint an inaccurate picture when measuring a site's strength. Instead, looking at the number of unique linking domains will give you a much better idea of how difficult it will be to compete with a site in the search results. Google places a high emphasis on unique linking domains, so you should, too.

The best way to get this figure is to use a tool called Open Site Explorer. Developed by a company called SEOMoz, Open Site Explorer provides a number of valuable SEO metrics and data. For full functionality, you'll need to purchase a paid membership but it's possible to get the metric we want - "Linking Root Domains" as labeled by the tool – for free.

When examining Google's search results, you'll want to look most carefully at the link metrics for the top few sites (#1 and #2 in Google) as well as the link metrics for the last site on the front page (#10 in Google). This will give you a rough idea of how much work is needed to not only rank #1, but also to simply make it on the first page of search results. The vast majority of searchers ends up clicking on one of the top ten results in Google, so you want to understand how difficult it will be to get your site ranked there.

Here's a quick cheat sheet for interpreting the number of unique linking domains. (These are only rough guidelines but should help you make sense of the numbers.)

0 to 50 Linking Root Domains: Will likely be on the low end for most worthwhile markets. Most sites with quality content and some focused marketing and SEO effort should be able to get 50 linking domains within a year.

50 to 250 Linking Root Domains: This is a more realistic range for top-ranked sites in decently sized niche markets. It may take a multi-year approach to build a backlink profile in this range, but it's feasible. A competitive landscape with this profile often offers the best work-to-reward ratio, especially for individual dropshipping entrepreneurs or very small teams.

250+ Linking Root Domains: Unless you're a talented marketer or SEO ninja, building up more than 250 unique links will take some serious time and commitment. It's not always a deal killer – just make sure you're ready to face some entrenched competition.

When determining a site's rank, Google doesn't just look at the number of links a site has. It also considers the quality of those links. So a link from Mike's Marshmallow Blog with five readers won't count anywhere close to as much as a link from The New York Times.

The metric Google uses to measure a page's authority is called PageRank. It's not the end-all-be-all of SEO metrics, but it's a quick way to get an idea of how important Google thinks a page is. As with unique linking sites, you can get a sense for how competitive a market is by looking at the PageRank for the homepages of top-ranked sites.

The easiest way to check PageRank is with a browser extension such as SearchStatus for Firefox. You can also check sites manually using sites like this one.

Here's A quick Way To Interpret Pagerank Readings For A Site's Homepage:

PageRank 1 to 2: A relatively small amount of authority. PageRank in this range for the top homepages likely indicates a relatively small market.

PageRank 3 to 4: A much more common range for highly ranked sites in competitive niche markets. It's not necessarily easy to reach this level of authority – but not impossible, either. Markets in this range usually offer the best work-to-reward range for individual drop shippers.

PageRank 4 to 5: A fairly high level of authority. To reach this level, you'll need to get numerous links from respected, authoritative sites, in addition to a fair number of other links.

PageRank 6+: You've got a full-time marketing and SEO department, right? Because you'll need them to compete in a market with sites like this.

Qualitative Metrics To Consider

Hard statistics like unique linking domains and PageRank can be helpful in determining how hard it will be to outrank competitors, but it's also very important to look at a few qualitative factors:

Site Quality and Usefulness – Visit the top-ranked sites for a market and put yourself in the shoes of a customer. Do they appear inviting and welcoming or old and outdated? Are the sites well-organized and easy to navigate or is it a struggle to even find the search box? Do they provide high-quality information and detailed product listings or do you have to squint to make out the grainy product images?

In short, how likely would you be to purchase from those sites? If you're blown away by the top sites in a market, it will be difficult to differentiate yourself and you may want to consider a different market. But if there's a lot of room for improvement – or, as we see it, opportunity to add value – that's a great sign.

Site Reputation and Customer Loyalty – An online business might have a solid reputation based on years of treating customers well, despite a drab design and outdated site. Alternatively, the most beautifully designed site might have a widespread reputation for awful customer service. It can be difficult to judge a book by its cover.

Check with the Better Business Bureau to see if a company has a history of customer complaints. You'll also want to do a web search to see what people are saying on social media and in online forums and communities. If the top competitors are slacking in the service and satisfaction department, there might be an opening for a store with superior service.

An Important Note on

Search Results

When you perform a search, it's important to realize that Google personalizes the results you see based on your geographic location, your browsing history and other factors. When we're analyzing a market, we need to see unbiased results so we can understand the real competitive landscape. Also, if you're living outside the states but plan on selling to US customers you need access to the search results your US-based customers will see as those are the sites you'll be competing with.

There Are Two Ways To Get Around These Issues:

Incognito Search: If you use Chrome as a browser, you can browse the web 'Incognito'. In this mode, any personalized settings or browsing history will discarded so you can get an unbiased idea of how sites actually rank. You can start an Incognito browsing sessions by going to "File → New Incognito Window" or by clicking on the icon in the upper right hand corner of your browser and selecting "New Incognito Window". Other web browsers have similar 'hidden search' modes that will clear your browsing history.

Forcing Nation-Specific Results: If you'd like to see the results that appear for a nation other than your own, you can add a small amount of text to the end of the URL on a Google results page to get country specific results.

For example, if you were in the UK but wanted to see the search results being returned to searches in the US, you'd add the "&gl=us" parameter to the end of the URL on the search results page and press enter. Similarly, if you were in the US and wanted to get UK results you'd add "&gl=uk" to the end of the URL.

CHAPTER 5

FINDING AND WORKING WITH SUPPLIERS

Before searching for suppliers, it's critical to know how to differentiate between legitimate wholesale suppliers and retail stores posing as wholesale suppliers. A true wholesaler buys directly from the manufacturer and will usually be able to offer you significantly better pricing.

How To Spot Fake Dropshipping Wholesalers

Depending on where you're searching, you'll likely come across a large number of "fake" wholesalers. Unfortunately legitimate wholesalers are traditionally poor at marketing and tend to be harder to find. This results in the non-genuine wholesalers – usually just middle men – appearing more frequently in your searches, so you'll want to be cautious.

The following tactics will help you discern whether a wholesale supplier is legitimate:

They Want Ongoing Fees – Real wholesalers don't charge their customers a monthly fee for the privilege of doing business and ordering from them. If a supplier asks for a monthly membership or service fee, it's likely not legitimate.

It's important to differentiate here between suppliers and supplier directories. Supplier directories The following tactics will help you discern whether a wholesale supplier is legitimate:

They Want Ongoing Fees – Real wholesalers don't charge their customers a monthly fee for the privilege of doing business and ordering from them. If a supplier asks for a monthly membership or service fee, it's likely not legitimate.

It's important to differentiate here between suppliers and supplier directories. Supplier directories are directories of wholesale suppliers organized by product types or market and screened to ensure the suppliers are legitimate. Most directories will charge a fee – either one time or ongoing – so you shouldn't take this as a sign the directory itself is illegitimate.

They Sell to the Public – To get genuine wholesale pricing you'll need to apply for a wholesale account, prove you're a legitimate business and be approved before placing your first order. Any wholesale supplier that offers products to the general public at "wholesale prices" is just a retailer offering items at inflated prices.

But Here Are Some Legitimate Dropshipping Fees You'll Likely Encounter:

Per-Order Fees – Many dropshippers will charge a per-order drop shipping fee that can range from $2 to $5 or more, depending on the size and complexity of the items being shipped. This is standard in the industry, as the costs of packing and shipping individual orders are much higher than shipping a bulk order.

Minimum Order Sizes – Some wholesalers will have a minimum initial order size, which is the lowest amount you have to purchase for your first order. They do this in order to filter out window-shopping merchants that will waste their time with questions and small orders but won't translate into meaningful business.

If you're dropshipping, this could cause some complications. For example, what do you do if a supplier has a $500 minimum order, but your average order size is around $100? You don't want to pre-order $500 of product just for the privilege of opening a dropshipping account.

In this situation, it's best to offer to pre-pay the supplier $500 to build a credit with them to apply against your drop shipping orders. This allows you to meet the supplier's minimum purchase requirement (as you're committing to buy at least $500 in product) without having to place a single large order without any corresponding customer orders.

Finding Wholesale Suppliers

Now that you can spot a fraud from the real deal, it's time to start searching for suppliers! You can use a number of different strategies, some more effective than others. The methods below are listed in order of effectiveness and preference, with our favorite methods listed first:

Contact the Manufacturer

This is our favorite way to easily locate legitimate wholesale suppliers. If you know the product(s) you want to sell, call the manufacturer and ask for a list of its wholesale distributors. You can then contact these wholesalers to see if they dropship and inquire about setting up an account.

Since most wholesalers carry products from a variety of manufacturers, this strategy will allow you to quickly source a selection of products within the niche you're exploring. After making a couple of calls to the leading manufacturers in a niche, you'll quickly be able to identify the leading wholesalers in that market.

Use Oberlo - www.oberlo.com

Oberlo allows you to easily import products from suppliers directly into your Shopify store, and ship directly to your customers – all in just a few clicks.

Features:

 Import Products from Suppliers.

Fulfil Orders Automatically.

Inventory and Price Auto Updates.

Product Customization

Pricing Automations

List of all Oberlo Dropshipping features.

Search Using Google

Using Google to find high-quality suppliers may seem obvious, but there are a few rules to keep in mind:

You Have to Search Extensively – Wholesalers are terrible at marketing and promotion, and they're definitely not going to top the search results for "wholesale suppliers for product X." This means you'll likely have to dig through LOTS of search results – possibly hundreds – to find the wholesaler's website listed way down.

Don't Judge by the Website – Wholesalers are also notorious for having poorly designed '90s-style websites. So while a quality site may indicate a good supplier in some cases, many legitimate wholesalers have cringe-worthy homepages. Don't let the poor design scare you off.

Use Lots of Modifiers – Wholesalers aren't doing extensive SEO to ensure you find their websites, so you might need to try various search queries. Don't stop at just "[product] wholesaler." Try using modifiers such as "distributor," "reseller," "bulk," "warehouse" and "supplier."

Order From the Competition

If you're having a hard time locating a supplier, you can always use the old order-from-the-competition trick. Here's how it works: Find a competitor you think is dropshipping and place a small order with that company. When you receive the package, Google the return address to find out who the original shipper was. In some cases, it will be a supplier you can contact.

This is a tactic we've heard discussed by others but haven't used ourselves. And if you haven't been able to find a supplier using the other techniques discussed above, there might be a good reason (i.e., the market is too small, there's not enough demand to justify a supplier, etc.). So keep this technique in mind, but don't rely too heavily on it.

Attend A Trade Show

A trade show allows you to connect with all the major manufacturers and wholesalers in a niche. It's a great way to make contacts and research your products and suppliers all in one spot. This only works if you've already selected your niche and/or product, and it isn't feasible for everyone. But if you have the time and money to attend, it's a great way to get to know the manufactures and suppliers in a market.

Directories

One of the most common questions aspiring ecommerce entrepreneurs ask is: Should I pay for a supplier directory?

A supplier directory is a database of suppliers that's organized by market, niche or product. Many directories employ some sort of screening process to ensure the suppliers listed are genuine wholesalers. Most are run by for-profit companies who charge a fee for access to their directory.

While membership directories can be helpful, especially for brainstorming ideas, they are by no means necessary. If you already know the product or niche you want to sell, you should be able to find the major suppliers in your market with a bit of digging and the techniques discussed above. Plus, once you start your business you likely won't need to revisit the directory unless you need to find suppliers for other products.

That said, supplier directories are a convenient way to quickly search for and/or browse a large number of suppliers in one place and are great for brainstorming ideas for products to sell or niches to enter. If you're short on time and are willing to spend the money, they can be a helpful tool.

There are a number of different supplier directories, and a comprehensive review of all of them is beyond the scope of this guide. Instead, we've highlighted some of the most well-known supplier directories online. Please note we are not endorsing any of these directories, we're simply providing you with some options.

Worldwide Brands

Quick Stats:

Established 1999

Thousands of wholesalers

Over 10 million products

Price: $299 for a lifetime membership

Worldwide Brands is one of the oldest and best-known supplier directories. It advertises that it only includes suppliers that meet a set of guidelines to ensure legitimate, quality wholesalers.

We've used the directory in the past to find legitimate wholesalers and to brainstorm niche ideas – and found it useful. Though the directory is missing some suppliers we've worked with, it does include a large collection of legitimate wholesalers. If you want lifetime access to a quality directory and are comfortable with a larger one-time payment, Worldwide Brands is a safe bet.

SaleHoo

Quick Stats:

Established 2005

Over 8,000 suppliers

Price: $67 per year

The SaleHoo supplier directory lists more than 8,000 bulk-purchase and dropshipping suppliers, and seems to cater heavily to merchants on eBay, and Amazon.

Although we've never used SaleHoo to source products, its $67 annual price is one of the most compelling values among supplier directories and includes a 60-day money-back guarantee. If you're comfortable paying an annual membership – or only need to use a directory temporarily - SaleHoo might be worth a look.

Doba

Quick Stats:

Established 2002

165 suppliers

Over 1.5 million products

Price: $60 per month

Instead of simply listing suppliers, Doba's service integrates with dropshippers (hence why they only have 165 suppliers) allowing you to place orders with multiple warehouses using its centralized interface. Membership also includes a Push-to-Marketplace tool that automates the process of listing items on eBay.

Doba's centralized system offers more convenience then the other directories which is why we imagine the $60 / month fee is significantly higher than other prices. If you place a high value on convenience and can find the products you want among their suppliers, Doba's interface may be worth the cost.

However, if you can identify quality suppliers on your own and don't mind working with them directly, you'll be able to save around $700 / year. If there are only a few key suppliers in your niche – reducing the number of parties you have to coordinate with – this may be the way to go.

Wholesale Central

Quick Stats:

Established 1996

1,400 suppliers

740,000 products

Price: free

Unlike many other directories, there's no charge to search Wholesale Central for suppliers because it charges suppliers a fee to be listed and also displays ads on their site. They also claim to review and screen all suppliers to ensure they are legitimate and trustworthy.

It's difficult to argue with free, and there's no harm in browsing the listings at Wholesale Central, but you'll need to be a bit more discriminating. A number of the suppliers we found appeared to be retailers selling to the public at "wholesale" prices – not something a supplier would do when offering real wholesale pricing. So while we're sure there are genuine wholesale opportunities listed, you may want to be a little more thorough with your due diligence.

Before You Contact Suppliers

But before you start contacting companies, you'll want to have all your ducks in a row.

You Need to Be Legal – As we mentioned earlier, most legitimate wholesalers will require proof that you're a legal business before allowing you to apply for an account. Most wholesalers only reveal their pricing to approved customers, so you'll need to be legally incorporated before you'll get to see the kind of pricing you'll receive.

Bottom line? Make sure you're legally incorporated before contacting suppliers! If you're only looking to ask a few basic questions ("Do you drop ship?" "Do you carry brand X?"), you won't need to provide any documentation. But don't expect to launch without having your business properly set up.

Understand How You Appear – Wholesalers are constantly bombarded by people with "great business plans" who pepper them with questions, take up a lot time and then never order anything. So if you're launching a new business, be aware that many suppliers aren't going to go out of their way to help you get started.

Most will be happy to set you up with a dropshipping account if they offer it. But don't ask for discount pricing or spend hours tying up their sales representatives on the phone before you've made a single sale. It will quickly earn you a bad reputation and hurt your relationship with the supplier.

If you do need to make special requests (say, trying to convince a supplier to dropship when it normally doesn't), you need to build credibility. Be definitive about your business plans ("We ARE launching this site on January 20) instead of using flaky rhetoric ("I'm thinking about maybe launching a business sometime soon"). And be sure to communicate any professional successes you've had in the past – especially with sales and marketing – that will help you with your new venture.

You need to convince suppliers that the inconvenience of accommodating your special request(s) will pay off down the road when you become successful and start bringing them a ton of business.

Don't Be Afraid of the Phone – One of the biggest fears people have when it comes to suppliers is simply picking up the phone and making the call. For many, this is a paralyzing prospect. You might be able to send emails for some issues, but more often than not you'll need to pick up the phone to get the information you need.

The good news is that it's not as scary as you might think. Suppliers are accustomed to having people call them, including newbie entrepreneurs. You're likely to get someone who's friendly and more than happy to answer your questions. Here's a tip that will help you, simply write out your questions ahead of time. It's amazing how much easier it is to make the call when you've got a list of pre-written questions to ask.

How to Find Good Suppliers

Like most things in life, suppliers are not all created equally. In the world of dropshipping – where the supplier is such a critical part of your fulfillment process – it's even more important to make sure you're working with top-notch players.

Great Suppliers Tend To Have Many Of The Following 6 Attributes:

Expert Staff And Industry Focus

Top-notch suppliers have knowledgeable sales representatives who really know the industry and their product lines. Being able to call a representative with questions is invaluable, especially if you're launching a store in a niche you're not overly familiar with.

Dedicated Support Representatives

Quality dropshippers should assign you an individual sales representative responsible for taking care of you and any issues you have. We've dealt with wholesalers that don't assign specific representatives and we hate it. Problems take a lot longer to resolve, and we usually have to nag people to take care of an issue. Having a single supplier contact who's responsible for solving your issues is really important.

Invested In Technology

While there are plenty of good suppliers with outdated websites, a supplier that understands the benefits of – and invests heavily in – technology is usually a pleasure to work with. Features such as real-time inventory, a comprehensive online catalog, customizable data feeds and an online searchable order history are pure luxury for online merchants and can help you streamline your operations.

Can Take Orders Via Email

This may sound like a minor issue, but having to call every order in – or manually place it on the website – makes processing orders significantly more time-intensive.

Centrally Located

If you're in a large country like the United States, it's beneficial to use a centrally located dropshipper, as packages can reach more than 90% of the country within 2 to 3 business days. When a supplier is located on one of the coasts, it can take more than a week for orders to be shipped across the country. Centrally located suppliers allow you to consistently promise faster delivery times, potentially saving you money on shipping fees.

Organized And Efficient

Some suppliers have competent staff and great systems that result in efficient and mostly error-free fulfillment. Others will botch every fourth order and make you want to tear your hair out. The trouble is, it's difficult to know how competent a supplier is without actually using it.

Although it won't give you a complete picture, placing a few small test orders can give you a great sense of how a supplier operates. You can see:

 How they handle the order process

How quickly the items ship out

How rapidly they follow up with tracking information and an invoice

The quality of the pack job when the item arrives

Your Options On Paying Suppliers

The vast majority of suppliers will accept payment in one of two ways:

Credit Card

When you're starting out, most suppliers will require you to pay by credit card. Once you've established a thriving business, paying with credit cards is often still the best option. They're not only convenient (no need to write checks regularly), but you can rack up a LOT of rewards points/frequent flier miles. Because you're buying a product for a customer who has already paid for it on your website, you can rack up a high volume of purchases through your credit card without having to incur any actual out-of-pocket expenses.

Net Terms

The other common way to pay suppliers is with "net terms" on invoice. This simply means that you have a certain number of days to pay the supplier for the goods you've purchased. So if you're on "net 30" terms, you have 30 days from the date of purchase to pay your supplier – by check or bank draw – for the goods you bought.

Usually, a supplier will make you provide credit references before offering net payment terms because it's effectively lending you money. This is a common practice, so don't be alarmed if you have to provide some documentation when paying on net terms.

CHAPTER 6

THE KEY ELEMENTS OF SUCCESS

Discussing everything from the fundamentals of dropshipping to the intricacies of picking a niche and running your business. By now, you should have enough of a foundation to confidently get started researching and launching your own dropshipping business.

With so much to consider, it's easy to get overwhelmed and lose track of what's really important. That's why we created this list of the crucial elements to success. These are the core "must-do" actions that will make or break your new venture. If you can successfully execute these, you'll be able to get a lot of other things wrong and still have a great chance at success.

1. Add Value

Having a solid plan for how you can add value to your customers is the most crucial success factor. This is important for all businesses, but much more so in the world of dropshipping, where you'll be competing with legions of other "me too" shops carrying similar products.

With dropshipping, it's easy to think you're selling customers a product. But successful small merchants understand that it's not only the product they offer – they're selling insights, information and solutions. You think you're an ecommerce merchant but you're also in the information business.

So how are you going to add value and help solve problems for your customers? If you're struggling to answer this question for a given niche, you may want to consider picking a different market.

If you're not able to add value through quality information and guidance, the only thing you're left to compete on is price. While this has been a successful strategy for Walmart, it's not going to help you build a successful drop shipping business.

2. Focus on Marketing and SEO

Coming in a close second to adding value as a key success factor is being able to drive traffic to your new site. The #1 problem and frustration new ecommerce merchants face is a lack of traffic to their websites. Too many merchants slave away for months on the perfect site only to launch it to a world that has no idea it exists.

Marketing and driving traffic is absolutely essential to the success of your business and is difficult to outsource well, especially if you have a small budget and are bootstrapping your business. You need to take the personal initiative to develop your own SEO, marketing, outreach and guest posting skills.

This is particularly crucial during the first 6 to 12 months, when no one knows who you are. Following your site launch, you need to dedicate at least 75% of your time on marketing, SEO and traffic generation for at least 4 to 6 months – that's right, 4 to 6 months! Once you've established a solid marketing foundation, you can scale back and coast a bit on the work you put in. But early on, it's impossible to place too much emphasis on marketing.

If you're not a marketing or SEO expert yet, the following resources and blogs are a great way to get started:

SEO Resources:

SEOmoz – One of the most popular SEO communities online. Their beginners guide to SEO is a particularly great resource for those starting out.

SeachEngineLand – Extremely prolific SEO blog, with dozens of new posts each day.

SEOBook – A popular SEO blog and the home of a paid private community for SEO professionals.

Distilled – This marketing and SEO agency has a top-notch blog and a number of quality training courses and guides, many of which are free.

Marketing Resources:

 Hubspot Blog – Advice on everything inbound marketing related, from driving traffic with email to social media tips.

Seth Godin's Blog – Solid high-level advice on marketing and building an audience.

Burst Free Product Photos - High-quality product images for popular dropshipping products.

QuickSprout – A blog by well-known entrepreneur Neil Patel dedicated largely to marketing, SEO and traffic generation.

KissMetrics Blog – In-depth marketing posts with a slant toward analytics, usability and conversion.

SparringMind – How to use behavioral psychology to help influence customers and market your business.

CopyBlogger – Content marketing tips with an emphasis on writing effective, compelling copywriting.

Mixergy – Interviews with successful entrepreneurs in the technology and online fields. Not focused exclusively on marketing, but lots of applicable information for aspiring entrepreneurs including marketing and early-stage advice.

Ecommerce Marketing Resources:

Shopify Blog – A comprehensive ecommerce blog with frequent posts on how to effectively promote and market your online store.

ecommerceFuel – Tips from an active ecommerce entrepreneur on how to found, grow and market online stores. Written specifically for individual store owners and smaller stores.

3. Specialize!

Almost every successful dropshipping store we encounter has one thing in common: It specializes in a certain product or niche. The more that stores specialize, the more successful they tend to be.

You don't want to just sell backpacks. You want to sell backpacks designed for around-the-world travelers obsessed with lightweight gear.

You don't want to just sell security camera equipment. You want to focus on security systems for gas stations.

Many think narrowing their focus limits their potential customer base and will cost them sales. Just the opposite is true! Specializing allows you to communicate more effectively with your customers, stand out more easily from the competition and compete against a smaller field. Specializing is rarely a bad move to make in a dropshipping venture.

If you're launching a store in a new niche you probably won't know what segment of your customers to focus on – and that's OK. But as you gain experience with your customers you should identify the segment that's the most profitable and that allows you to add the most value. Then, try to position your business to focus exclusively on those customers' needs and problems. You'll be amazed at how your conversion rates skyrocket even if you're charging a premium price.

Remember: If everyone is your customer, then no one is. Specialization makes it easier to differentiate yourself, charge a premium price and concentrate your marketing efforts more effectively.

4. Have a Long-Term Perspective

Building a dropshipping business is like building anything else of value: It takes a significant level of commitment and investment over time. Yet for some reason people assume they can build a passive six-figure income with dropshipping after a few months of part-time work. That's just not the way it works.

it will realistically take at least a year to build a business that generates an average full-time income.

It's also important to understand that the first few months are the most difficult. You'll struggle with doubts, run into issues with your website and will likely have an underwhelming website launch that generates zero sales. Understand that this is normal! Rome wasn't built in a day, and neither were any successful dropshipping businesses.

If you mentally prepare for a challenging beginning and don't expect to get rich overnight, you'll be much more likely to stick with your business until it becomes a success.

5. Offer Outstanding Service

The Internet has always been a fairly transparent place, but the recent rise of social media has made your business reputation even more important to your success online. If you don't treat your customers well, they'll often let the entire world know – including many potential customers.

The biggest customer service risk for dropshipping merchants is having tunnel vision on per-order profits and losses when fulfillment issues go awry.

it's critical to accept that dropshipping can get messy, that you'll be paying to clean up some messes, and that you shouldn't always try to pass these on to your customer. If you aren't occasionally losing money on individual orders to make customers happy, you're probably not providing very good service.

Having happy customers is some of – if not THE – best marketing you can do. As is true in all businesses, it's much easier to make a sale to a satisfied customer than to try to convince a new prospect to buy. If you treat your customers exceptionally well, they're likely to spread the word and refer others your way. With top-notch service, you can build a business where repeat customers generate much of your revenue.

Making customer service a priority set your dropshipping business up for success, so ensure it's a priority from the outset.

6. Don't Get Hung Up on the Details

Don't focus too much on the details. Your company name, logo, theme or email marketing service aren't going to determine your success.

What makes a business successful are the things we just talked about: adding value, marketing, outstanding customer service, specializing and a long-term commitment. Still, new merchants will spend weeks – sometimes months – struggling to make a decision between two shopping carts or providers. That's valuable time better spent developing the core aspects of the business.

Do your research and make an informed decision, but don't let small decisions paralyze you.

7. The Most Important Step

The most important step – the one that most people never take – is to actually get started building your business! This is the hardest thing for most people and it's usually a result of fear and uncertainty.

It's a common misconception that successful entrepreneurs have a rock-solid certainty about their business at the outset. When you dig a little deeper, you'll find that most had fears and reservations about how things would turn out. Yet they moved forward with their plan despite these doubts.

If you're serious about building your own dropshipping business, you'll need to do the same. Do your research, evaluate your options and then move forward with that information in spite of your fears and reservations. It's what entrepreneurs do. Start now.

Share on Twitter

Share on Facebook

Share on Google+

Share on LinkedIn

Made in United States
North Haven, CT
20 October 2022

25689910R00054